POETRY: THE TRUE EXPRESSIONS

POETRY: THE TRUE EXPRESSIONS

April Joy Smith

Copyright © 2000 by April Joy Smith.

Softcover   0-7388-4321-0

All rights reserved. No part of this book may be reproduced or transmitted in any form or by any means, electronic or mechanical, including photocopying, recording, or by any information storage and retrieval system, without permission in writing from the copyright owner.

This book was printed in the United States of America.

To order additional copies of this book, contact:
Xlibris Corporation
1-888-7-XLIBRIS
www.Xlibris.com
Orders@Xlibris.com

CONTENTS

Changes of the Seasons 11
A Day at the Beach 12
The Drought 13
Hurricane Bonnie 14
Jail Life at the S.P.C.A. 15
Life 16
Paradise 17
World Peace 18
The Tornado 19
Thunder And Lightning 20
Spring is Here 21
A Rainbow 22
The Obituary 23
Homicide or Suicide? 24
The Hanging 25
The Graveyard 26
The Funeral 27
The Deadly Baseball Game 28
Death 29
A Special Friend 30
She Made Me See 31
What is a Friend? 32
My True Love 33
My True Hero 34
My Friends 35
Mandy 36
Get Well Soon 37
Grease 38

A Great Friend	39
Forever With You	40
Friends	41
Forever	42
A Scary Day At School	43
A Stranger	44
School: A Place	45
Who Can	46
Halloween	47
The Mysterious Night	48
The Ghost	49
Drunk Driving	50
The Accident	51
The Prowler	52
Boys	53
Children	54
Day Dreams	55
Genuardi's	56
Graduation	57
Two Greats	58
Observations at 4:00 a.m.	59
I WishI Could be Like You	60
Gone, but Not Forgotten	61
Francis	62
Don't	63
The Best Friend	64
A Best Friend Never Forgotten	66
The End	67
The End	68
A New Friend	69
A Special Person	70
My Worst Fear	71
The Worst Night	72
Adrienne and Ruthie	73
Colleen	74
The Heart	75

Hidden Love	76
Pain	77
Jack	78
Love	79
All Night Party	80
Are Feelings Wrong?	81
Summer	82
Barney	83
The Best Present	84
I Remember You Always	85
Sue	86
True or Not?	87
A New Beginning	88
Far Apart, but Closer Than Ever	89
Redners	90
Pressure	91
The Ocean	92
Things Happen For a Reason	93
Popeye	94
There Are Some Things	95
Always in my Heart	96
Express Shop Adventures	97
The Real World	98
The Millenium	99
I Wish	100
Enough or Not?	101
A Birthday Wish	102
Goodbye, Again	103
The Brighter Side of a Bad Night	104
A Special Person	105
I'm Sorry	106
Sue	107
Bad Luck	108
I Wish You Were Here	109
Sometimes	110
Andy Kauffman	111

I would like to dedicate this book to a couple of people. The first person I am dedicating it to is Miss Shields. I would never be where I am now if it wasn't for her. And to Mrs. Conrad for believing in me and my writing. I also could not have completed this without the faith and inspiration of Sue McCandless, Shawn Powell, and Christina. The final person this book is going out to is my best friend Stephanie Smith. She stood by me for six years, and even more. She has given me even more reason to believe in myself. A friend like her makes everything in life better.

CHANGES OF THE SEASONS

Sleet, hail, and ice on the ground,
the snow is blowing all around.
Children build snowmen of all heights,
while others are having snowball fights.
All of this stuff is a winter trend,
before they knew it, it had come to an end.
Short sleeve shirts are now out,
flowers popping up all about.
The smell of fresh grass in the air,
better enjoy it while it's there.
It was a good season, but we lost a friend,
Spring has now come to an end.
Yellow jackets and wasps, the bees are near,
because Summer time is now here.
The sound of people splashing in pools,
school is out, no more rules.
This was too good a season to even last,
Fall is here now, summer is past.
School clothes are out in the store,
back to school to learn some more.
The sound of laughing and talking to everyone,
no more beaches, or lying in the sun.
The cycle will start back up and then,
over it will start again and again.

A DAY AT THE BEACH

Walking on the board walk, lying in the sun,
going down the water slides and having lots of fun.
Running across the hot, hot sand,
couples holding each other's hand.
Swimming in the water with the fish,
hearing the sound of the water go swish.
Children build sandcastles all around,
or bury their parents in the ground.
Beach pails, shovels, balls, and tools,
the best part is, there are no rules.
Getting a tan, or getting a sunburn,
watching the merry go-rounds as they turn.
Running, swimming, relaxing, or even if you sleep,
this is a memory you will want to keep.
The water will come in, and then go away,
it's in a pattern just like a sway.
When it's time to pack and go,
you'll be back again, that you know.
When you come back, it will be the same,
but it was so special; you will give it a name.

THE DROUGHT

The sun beat down from way up high,
but the ground needed water because it was dry.
The grass was no longer green, it was brown,
we really needed days and days of a good pour down.
No one was allowed to wash their car or water their lawn,
not until it rained a lot and the drought was gone.
The farmers were in trouble with the corn and the crops,
the needed at least a week of rain, not a couple of drops.
Everyone had to be careful, a fire could start fast,
there was just no telling how long the drought would last.
The farmers waited patiently for the rain to come around,
and the corn and crops rose nicely from the wet ground.

HURRICANE BONNIE

Most vacations were ruined on that fateful day,
a big storm was coming, Bonnie was on the way.
All swimmers were ordered to leave the beach,
no one knew how far Bonnie would reach.
The surf in the water was extremely high,
if anyone went out too far, they would die.
As the water pushed harder, it sounded like thunder,
and the force of it pulled one guy under.
The sound of hammering nails could be heard,
especially when they got the final word.
People were boarding their windows with wood,
everyone preparing for safety the best they could.
The winds picked up over 100 miles per hour,
and what exactly would Bonnie devour?
The rain came hard, hard as could be,
the sky was impossible to even see.
The storm did damage, but not a lot,
where would it go next, to what spot?

JAIL LIFE AT THE S.P.C.A.

Meows, meows, meows everywhere.
Cats locked up in small cages.
No room to run,
no room to play.
It's like a jail.
They only get food and water.
They wait patiently
for that one person to adopt them.
A person comes and
the cats rub around the cage.
They meow because they want out.
If by a certain amount of time
they are not freed,
They will be put to sleep.
Every day a cat is adopted and,
it will show love towards its master,
because it is happy to be out of jail.

LIFE

Life is the most beautiful thing,
to wake up and hear the birds sing.
To breathe every breath of air,
to know that people really care.
Having the sun shine on your face,
knowing you have a protected place.
To be able to see the flowers and trees,
and even the butterflies and the bees.
Having friends and love all around,
this is the best thing that can be found.
And when you are in bed late at night,
dreaming good dreams while you're tucked in tight.
So, when this daily cycle starts over the next day,
you'll realize there's nothing better than life, no way.

PARADISE

I woke up one day, and what did I see?
something was different, what could it be?
Everything was changed, nothing was the same,
was this a joke, or some kind of a game?
The sun was out, not a cloud in the sky,
not a drop of rain came from way up high.
There was no fighting, everyone getting along,
they were doing right things, nothing wrong.
There were no hospitals because no one was ill,
no vaccines were needed, not even a pill.
I stood there, what I had seen I couldn't believe,
and I wanted to stay here, never wanted to leave.
What caused this change, I really don't know,
but I'll be here forever, I'll never go.

WORLD PEACE

Too much violence, murders, and hate,
no more murders, or violence would be great.
If everyone would think before they do,
everyone would be better for me and you.
There should be one side, not two or three,
imagine what our world could possibly be.
No more fights, everyone getting along,
openly admitting when they are wrong.
All the war was, was a way out,
easier to fight, than to walk away and go about.
You can't buy world peace, there is no price,
yeah, world peace would be great, it would be nice.
World peace is a dream, but it can be true,
if you help me and I help you.

THE TORNADO

The sky grew dark as the rain poured down,
there was fear in the air and panic in the town.
Then came a loud crash out of the sky,
around, you could hear babies begin to cry.
Then the hail came down from above,
big enough to be caught with a baseball glove.
The wind picked up stronger and stronger,
the town wouldn't be the same for much longer.
Then it came, the tornado ripped through,
picking up houses, trees, and cars too.
It spun around, throwing things everywhere,
all the trees were gone, the ground was bare.
The tornado left as fast as it came,
the town was definitely not the same.
Many people were hurt, five dead,
some stayed in the town, some fled.
The next day came, a stillness in the air,
but the damage had been done, the fear still there.

THUNDER AND LIGHTNING

The rain comes into the dark night,
nothing can be seen, not even a light.
There is a loud bang that makes the ground shake,
and pretty soon everyone is wide awake.
The next bang sounds like a gun, what a noise!
the children are crying, the girls and the boys.
The sky lights up pink and blue,
in the window the lightning comes through.
The lightning strikes down to the ground,
everyone is hiding, not a brave soul can be found.
What a scary sound, what a scary night!
no one will ever get to sleep tonight.
Then it happens, the worst thing of all,
the lighting comes in the house through the wall.
The people were lucky it didn't strike a wire,
it could have killed someone or started a fire.
Soon it goes far, far away,
but the fear in the air will always stay.

SPRING IS HERE

Winter is gone, Spring is here,
time for the children to let out their cheer.
The sky is bright, the grass is green,
no signs of snow or ice can be seen.
The birds are out chirping away,
time to start a new Spring day.
No more heavy coats, gloves or hats,
it's time to get out the ball and bats.
The sun is shining brightly in the sky,
so take a walk or find a place to relax and lie.
The trees are sprouting up nice and tall,
the leaves are back on and will not soon fall.
Red tulips, roses, daises, and flowers,
and the next month will bring April showers.
The smell of fresh grass is in the air,
better enjoy it while it's there.
Walks through the park, riding a bike,
this is what Spring is really like.
So, get up and get out,
this is what Spring is all about.

A RAINBOW

It was raining hard, hard as could be,
but when it was over, what did I see?
The sky started to show a little light,
and then there was something shining bright.
The sun was not the only thing shining down,
a mix of bright colors was also around.
Red, orange, yellow, blue, and green,
the most beautiful thing to ever be seen.
It doesn't sit too high, or too low,
what else could it be, but a rainbow.
The legend of this that was told,
is at the end of it is a pot of gold.
When a storm comes, and it's really bad,
the rainbow afterwards will make you less sad.

THE OBITUARY

Her name was in the paper, in big dark bold,
and under it was a story that was told.
The story was the talk of the town,
but did it make people smile, or make them frown?
It's a biography, so they should smile, right?
no, because it's not a biography, cheery and bright.
The story is about a girl who is no longer alive,
she got killed by a car when she was just five.
So what is this story, what could it possibly be?
it is this poor girls' obituary.

HOMICIDE OR SUICIDE?

It was a rainy, stormy, dark night,
there was thunder, lightning, and lots of fright.
In the distance, an object lay on the street,
it looked like it had a head and two feet.
It was a body, and it didn't move,
why would someone kill her, what was there to prove?
There was blood all around, she was shot in the head,
and next to the body lay the gun with the deadly lead.
There were no witnesses, none at all,
phoning her parents would be the worst call.
But, there was one thing left about the day she died,
they think maybe she wasn't murdered, but it was suicide.
To this day, the death is a mystery,
homicide or suicide, both could be.

THE HANGING

A girl disappeared one dark night,
her family knew something wasn't right.
From the closet came a loud bang,
they all jumped then when the phone rang.
The police searched everywhere, they had no clue,
there was nothing anyone could possibly do.
The next noise was loud, loud as could be,
but they were afraid to look at what they'd see.
Slowly they opened the door to take a look,
and there hung the girl on a rope from the hook.

THE GRAVEYARD

The night was dark with a chill in the air,
a lot of places are scary, but especially there.
There were trees and leaves all around,
and grave stones planted in the ground.
Empty holes, not a lot, but some,
waiting for the next person to come.
The hole is the perfect width, the perfect size,
and once you are put in it, you will never rise.
Some say it's a resting place, some say no,
and we'll never find out, even those who go.

THE FUNERAL

The morgue keeps the body put away and cold,
until the funeral day when a prayer will be told.
The hearse comes and takes the body away,
it will be buried deep the very next day.
The flowers are in the casket all around,
soon it will be placed down in the ground.
The people come, the eerie music begins to play,
nothing no one can do, nothing anyone can say.
The body just lies there, looking peacefully at rest,
it was made up to look young and the very best.
The prayer is told, everyone perfectly quiet, being brave,
but now it's the final stop, the trip to the grave.
Everyone gets a glance at the body just once more,
and they all know what the hole is there for.
The casket was lowered and dirt was thrown on top,
and no one would ever forget her, they would never stop.

THE DEADLY BASEBALL GAME

One day there was a baseball game at the Vet,
none of the audience had arrived yet.
When they got there, nothing would be the same,
no one would get out after this baseball game.
There was just something here that wasn't right,
and this would soon be an unforgettable night.
The first couple of pitches left a chill in the air,
but the audience better pay attention, and be aware.
About half way through the game, the truth came out,
there was a maniac in the stands roaming about.
No one knew who he was or where he had come from,
but when they found out he was a maniac they got numb.
One person tried to find the guy and put up a fight,
until the bomb went off and blew up everyone in sight.
It was an unforgettable night for whoever survived,
it was only the maniac, who left after he had arrived.

DEATH

She stands out in the middle of the street,
waiting for her chance for her and death to meet.
Why she's doing this, no one knows,
a car is coming, a loud horn blows.
The girl is pronounced dead,
there is blood coming from her mouth and head.
How could this girl get taken away?
but now it's time for the funeral and burial day.
Her family and friends, they all came,
now nothing would ever be the same.
Now the casket is lowered in the ground,
everyone is standing there looking down.
There are flowers all around the grave,
but now they all have to be brave.
They all still wonder why,
but now it's time to say good-bye.

A SPECIAL FRIEND (DEDICATED TO JANET LIGHT)

You have been having some problems, that I know,
but I am here for you to help you continue to go.
You are not having the best of luck, what can I say,
I am always your friend, day by day.
I know a lot doesn't go right, things go wrong,
but I know you will make it because you are strong.
Anytime you need me, I will always be there,
even though I may not show it, I really do care.
You are such a special friend with a very important part,
you will always have a special place in my heart.
Thank you, your friendship is so precious to me,
without a friend like you, I don't know where I'd be.

SHE MADE ME SEE (DEDICATED TO JANET LIGHT)

At first I wondered, would I fit in, should I try?
would she like me for who I am, or should I lie?
I could tell she was a great person and friend,
for her to like me, would I have to follow a trend?
At first I didn't know her very well,
but she was a nice person as far as I could tell.
Sooner than I expected, the truth came out,
she was what a true friend was all about.
I was afraid I would do or say something wrong,
but it was just me being paranoid all along.
Now, my friend has made me see,
only have friends who like me for me.

WHAT IS A FRIEND?

A friend is someone who you can talk to,
A friend is someone who will always care.
A friend will stick by you and see you through,
A friend will never leave and be right there.
A friend is a person who means a lot,
A friend will never lead you the wrong way.
A friend will always have that special spot,
A friend will know just the right thing to say.
A friend can be older or even younger,
A friend plays a very important part.
A friend lifts you up and makes you stronger,
A friend will forever be in your heart.
A friend will not make you follow a trend,
A good friendship will last until the end.

MY TRUE LOVE (DEDICATED TO FRANCIS FIZZAROTTI)

Nothing was going right, everything went wrong,
but that all changed when you came along.
As I stood there getting ready to ask you out,
I knew it would work, there was never a doubt.
Every time I see you, my heart skips a beat,
one look from you and my body fills with heat.
You're what I've been waiting for, like a dream come true,
and the only thing I can say is, I will forever love you.
I think of you every second, every minute of every day,
I will never leave you, there is no possible way.
I love every minute we spend together, day and night,
especially when I'm in your arms and you hold me tight.
I love you so much, this for sure I know,
and we will never part, our hearts will help us grow.

MY TRUE HERO (DEDICATED TO MIKE SMITH)

I know a lot of hard working people around,
but there's one special guy who can easily be found.
He does not play a sport but is still well known,
he was special to me when he was little, and now since he's grown.
He is always helping out everyone that he possibly can,
the sports teams, Mr. McDaniel, and even trainer Dan.
Even I need his help when I'm doing my homework at night,
I get frustrated and he calms me down so then I do it right.
Everyone knows my brother, everyone knows Mike,
but for the good things he does, and that's what I really like.
Mike has accomplished more than anyone I know,
he is always ready to move, always on the go.
Mike is one of the people who makes me proud,
and I'm not afraid to say it to one person or a crowd.
Mike is my brother, and he is also my friend,
he will always be my hero from now until the end.

MY FRIENDS (DEDICATED TO KELLY, JEWEL, AND DANIELLE)

A good friend to everyone I tried to be,
and in return I was sent not one but three.
I didn't know why, I just wasn't sure,
but you were the friends I was looking for.
Just when I thought no one else could care,
you always seemed to be right there.
Such good friends I never thought I would find,
and that to me makes you all one of a kind.
Sometimes I know I get confused about a whole lot,
but I know I am thankful for the friends I have got.
I know I get into bad moods, and try to push you away,
but being my friend means more than I could ever say.
From start to finish, from beginning to end,
I will always be proud to call you my friend.

MANDY (DEDICATED TO MANDY OLEARSKY)

She is one of the most dedicated workers at the store,
she always does what is expected and then much more.
She comes to work on time and is never late,
she takes care of the customers so they don't have to wait.
She talks to the customers, making them less bored,
Mandy's reputation as a great person has really soared.
She helps customers and workers in every possible way,
she tries her best, and succeeds day by day.
Mandy is also a mother, a wife, and a friend,
she will always listen to your stories from beginning to end.
Mandy knows when to get serious and when to have fun,
she deserves employee of the month, everything she's done.

GET WELL SOON (DEDICATED TO AMY KASOPSKY)

You have been sick for the past week or so,
I am thinking of you, just so you know.
I was worried about you when you had the flu,
I would make it go away if there were something I could do.
I feel bad when you are down and sick like this,
you are out of work a lot, which you don't like to miss.
I wish I could just flash you a smile and make it go away,
but I can't, so I'll just try to brighten up your day.
I am no doctor, but I will try my very best,
to make sure you are well again from plenty of rest.
Hopefully soon you will be up and around,
reading this poem should help you when you are down.

GREASE

It was a summer day,
when they met at the beach,
they had found a love, they
thought they could never reach.
But then she moved away.
Summer was over and
school had begun.
He was lonely, but he had
his own group of friends.
Then she came back and
he acted like a different person.
He was showing off
for his friends.
Deep down, this boy
still loved her very much.
They got back together, and
went to the movies.
They had a date to meet
at the carnival that night.
When he got there,
he was in shock.
She had made a great
change in herself.
His friends and her friends
never really got along.
At the end, they came together
just like friends.

A GREAT FRIEND (DEDICATED TO ADRIENNE BAMBI)

Sometimes I go to work and I'm having a bad day,
everything goes wrong, nothing seems to go my way.
You are one of those people who smiles a whole lot,
and I know you are one friend I have definitely got.
When I come to work, I look forward to seeing your friendly face,
you never put me down, or make me feel out of place.
I love bagging for you, it is my pleasure,
your friendship to me will always be a treasure.
Thank you for everything you have done and will do,
all of your friendliness will be returned to you.
Keep this poem, with it you should never part,
because everything I said came straight from my heart.

FOREVER WITH YOU (DEDICATED TO FRANCIS FIZZAROTTI)

You are always and forever on my mind,
there's no one like you, you're one of a kind.
When we're apart, no matter where you've been,
I can not wait until we are together again.
Every minute we spend together is precious to me,
together forever is what we were meant to be.
You are my guardian angel, my shining star,
I'll love you when you're near, I'll love you when you're far.
I love you so much from the bottom of my heart,
I could not stand it if we would ever part.
Forever and ever our love will last,
I am under your love spell that you have cast.

FRIENDS

Friends are special, they mean so much,
they've got that certain way, that magical touch.
Friends like you for who you are,
not because of your clothes, money, or car.
They stick by you through bad and good,
and treat you right, like any friend would.
Having only one good friend, don't even try,
what would happen if they would move away or even die?
In your life friends play a big part,
they will always and forever be in your heart.
Look around, look at yourself, look at me,
I've got a couple good friends, two or three.

FOREVER (DEDICATED TO SHAWN POWELL)

I went out with him for six years,
he stood by me and calmed my fears.
I loved him so much with all my heart,
and he promised me we would never part.
He loved me and would tell me every day,
he said he would never leave me, there was no way.
But, he later he started to act like he didn't love me,
why, what was the problem, what could it be?
It started to get worse, and went on for a while,
why would he ever put our love to a test, on a trial?
Then one day he was still acting like a jerk,
he came up to me and said it just wasn't going to work.
Standing there, I didn't know what to say,
this couldn't be happening, there was no way.
It had to be my fault, so what did I do?
what was the cause of us being through?
Then I realized it wasn't my fault, it wasn't me,
but that's even worse, I can't fix the way we use to be.
I tried to get him back, every minute, every hour,
but he won't come back, he acts like he has supreme power.
I still love him and I will never let him go,
I can't go on without him, that I know.
So, in my heart he will always stay,
I'll never stop loving him for one day.

A SCARY DAY AT SCHOOL

The school day began, but it was very strange,
in a split second all our lives could change.
There was a rumor in the school going around,
a bomb will blow up our school up, but no evidence was found,
It was all over the internet and our school,
whoever did this thought it was funny and cool.
The principles told us there was nothing to worry about,
but after all that was going on, we had a good reason to doubt.
I sat in class and watched the students leave and as they walked by,
I realized I had to get out, I was too young to die.
By the end of the day our school was still there,
but going back won't take the sense of fear from the air.

A STRANGER AT MY WINDOW

One night before I went to bed,
something was strange, the town was dead.
No sound could be heard, near, or far,
no trains, buses, not even a car.
I went to my window, there were two eyes,
what a shocking sight, what a big surprise!
He stared at me, his look was ice cold,
and said he would be back if I told.
Then he disappeared as fast as he came,
was he for real, or was this a game?
I didn't like this, not at all,
so I decided to give the police a call.
I opened the door, a cop I thought I would see,
it wasn't it was the same guy that was staring at me.
Then I started to shake and to scream,
and I woke up, it was just a dream.

SCHOOL: A PLACE FOR PEACE OR NOT?

There was a still peacefulness in the air,
everyone in class, the streets almost bare.
All of a sudden gun shots rang out,
all of the students tried to run and shout.
There were two suspects dressed in all black,
what could have possibly caused this attack?
One boy was shot in the back and the arm,
but a couple of students got out because of the alarm.
Another girl was shot nine times in the chest,
these two men took away their place of peace and rest.
By the time everything had come to a head,
a couple of students were found in the library dead.
The students were reunited with parents again,
there were mixed emotions that shouldn't have been.
These students had to go through this horrible day,
with help from friends they will be on their way.

WHO CAN YOU REALLY TRUST?

One day you meet your neighbor friend,
he's your age, right away you both mend.
You are both good friends through the years,
through the laughs and through the tears.
He is the sweetest person anyone could see,
he would never hurt anyone, not even a bee.
Friends from first through ninth grade,
he never got in trouble, he always obeyed.
But then they separated into a different school,
nothing changed between them, they were still cool.
Then an accident occurred one fateful day,
I was in shock and didn't know what to say.
The police and rescue people were all around,
and I couldn't believe what they had found.
My friend had beaten his dad with a bat in the head,
it was so bad that he probably would soon be dead.
A soon as he got to the hospital, he died,
all I could feel was sick deep inside.
What caused this accident, I don't know,
but I won't end our friendship, on it will still go.

HALLOWEEN

The children left the house to go trick or treating,
they didn't know who they would soon be meeting.
The sky was dark, but the night was clear,
they had no clue that danger was near.
They went to one house and got some candy,
everyone thought their costumes were dandy.
They wondered away and were all of a sudden alone,
far away with no cars, no help, and no phone.
Then they heard footsteps coming up from behind,
and they were scared to turn around at what they'd find.
They turned around and no one was there,
so they figured it was just a Halloween scare.
But they were still alone, wondering around,
was there any hope that the children would be found?
Then it started to rain, so up went their hoods,
but then they were grabbed an taken in the woods.
Their parents still look till this, in dark or light,
no one knows what happened to them on Halloween night.

THE MYSTERIOUS NIGHT

it was raining hard, not one light on the street,
In a distance you hear two running feet.
there was a man dressed in black hanging around,
he might have been the murderer that was never found.
Then he was chasing after a girl with a knife,
and was planning to take away her innocent life.
The body was found later, about an hour or so,
the guy was nowhere around, where did he go?
But, there is an ever bigger mystery about that night,
the coroner says she was strangled while putting up a fight.
The guy didn't have a rope, just a sharp knife,
so, who really did end this girl's life?
There was probably more than one guy,
but at the funeral, everyone asked why.
At the funeral, there was a guy with a can of Miller,
he looked so familiar, uh-oh it was the killer.
So, lock your doors tight before going to bed,
or he might come after you, and you'll end up dead.

THE GHOST

The old abandoned house stood on the corner of the street,
it use to be where the children would trick or treat.
Both the owners of the house got sick and died,
since then, no one has ever stepped one foot inside.
A boy got dared to go to the house and spend the night,
he was scared to go, he was filled with fright.
The boy decided to do it, he had to be brave and strong,
how many minutes or hours would he last, just how long?
He went to the house that night around nine,
he told himself he would be ok, he would be just fine.
The first thing he did was explore the halls,
and he found spiders and cobwebs on the walls.
Then a noise came from the attic, what a big surprise,
he was face to face with a ghost, with his two eyes.
He took off as fast as his two feet could go,
where he was now, he didn't know.
He finally found his way out of the nightmare,
but no one believed him, they didn't even care.
But, who was really the boy that came out,
it just may be the ghost now roaming about.

DRUNK DRIVING

The dead body was taken away,
everyone just stared with nothing to say.
The guy had crashed into a pole,
he was drunk and now he's paying the toll.
He guzzled down about eight beers,
now because of him everyone is in tears.
Control and vision played a big part,
this guy was stupid, he wasn't too smart.
The guy previously had a fight with his wife,
he went out and got drunk, didn't care about his life.
His friend gave a speech at the funeral that day,
his closing statement: drinking and driving isn't the way.

THE ACCIDENT

Loud screeching brakes, a loud piercing scream,
it's like a nightmare, it's a really bad dream.
All along the road lay pieces of glass,
will this nightmare ever end or pass?
But this is not a nightmare, it's real,
imagine how these people must feel.
Motionless bodies lay all around,
no noise is heard, not even a little sound.
No breath is left in them, they're dead,
mainly from the hemorrhage to their head.
Only two witnesses survived that fateful day,
and they told the story to make their pain go away.
What caused this accident, was someone drunk?
maybe someone was trying to be cool, like a punk.
Maybe someone was high on heroin or crack,
whatever it was, it won't bring the victims back.

THE PROWLER

What's that furry thing that runs around the house?
and will chase a bird, a squirrel, and even a mouse.
It sleeps during the day, and runs in the dark night,
its' tail gets bushy when it's filled with fright.
When it gets outside, be careful as can be,
it might sneak away and climb a tree.
The food it eats is canned or dried,
but it would love a fish, raw or fried.
This is the cleanest thing ever to be found,
even when there are two of them fighting on the ground.
A lot of fur, a lot of love, and a lot of care,
unless it dies, it will always be there.

BOYS

They get dirty fast outside,
they have a motorcycle to ride.
Out playing basketball or football,
pushing each other down so they fall.
Out all hours past the night,
and all they want to do is fight.
On a date, some are not gentlemen, some are,
most of them will try and impress you with a car.
The other boys will act like themselves, really try,
they won't wear jeans, they would wear a suit and tie.
No matter what they do, we love them anyway,
seeing their smiling faces every day.
They can bring out most of our joys,
so, what would we really do without boys?

CHILDREN

Playing in the park, going down the slides,
going to amusement parks, going on the rides.
Running through the yard, playing in the grass,
watching the grown ups and older people pass.
They scream for their parents when a bad storm hits,
and when they can't get what they want, throw fits.
They are scared of the dark, so they need a night light,
and want to stay up, so their bed times they fight.
Children show you the best possible form of love,
and you know they had to be sent from above.
It doesn't matter if there are a lot of them or a few,
because, without children, what would we do?

DAY DREAMS

She stares out the window into the day,
slowly her mind drifts far away.
Nothing can be seen, nothing at all,
not a sound can be heard, not even a call.
She is in another world, somewhere out there,
but what's going on around her, she's not aware.
The teacher calls her name, but she can't hear,
her many thoughts are there, but her mind is nowhere near.
Her mind is now back from far away,
and can now continue the rest of the day.
But will she go into another day dream?
and will her mind flow away like a stream?

GENUARDI'S

A job where you bag, cashier, and clean,
the customers are nice, not at all mean.
Weekends, weekdays, whatever they may be,
a lot of people like it there, especially me.
There is a lot of team work around the store,
it's the best thing in the world, who would want more?
Pushing carts, and bagging, bagging away,
I would love to do this every single day.
The friendliness of the people is everywhere,
and you have to be paying attention, being aware.
The hardest thing is when you are starting new,
it will seem as if everyone is staring at you.
But as time goes on, you will start to see,
this is the best place you could possibly be.
The workers are definitely liked a lot,
but don't start bagging and stay in one spot.
If you're outside, help the customers to their car,
even if it's close to the store, or very far.
Don't forget to smile and have a friendly voice,
so the next time they go shopping, Genuardi's is their choice.

GRADUATION

The excitement was building up inside of me,
success, hard work, and determination was the main key.
I stood on the top bleachers looking all the way down,
I had my cap, tassel, and my white graduation gown.
Then my name was called, my diploma in my hand,
there was a sound of applause, and the playing of the band.
That was it, for me school had finally come to an end,
one thing I did right was making every single friend.
I said my good-byes to those who meant so much,
but I knew I would see them again, we'd keep in touch.
Being out in the real world is a change and not always fun,
but I will change for me, not for anything or anyone.

TWO GREATS

Babe Ruth was a legend, part of everyone's heart and mind,
he was so great, there would never be another kind.
Then Sammy Sosa and Mark McGwire began playing,
people would soon be talking, what would they be saying?
There were a lot of hits and each one hard and good,
both players did the very best they possibly could.
No one knew exactly how good they would really get,
and they run fast, almost like a plane or a jet.
Then Mark and Sammy hit a homerun or two,
pretty soon it became definitely more than a few.
Then it was ten, fifteen, twenty, and then thirty,
baseball was their life, even if it meant getting dirty.
All of a sudden the numbers went up high,
as the homeruns soared way up to the sky.
The record would soon be broken, or tied,
and Mark did it first, and his mother cried.
The crowd went crazy, they cheered loud,
both of these men made the fans proud.
Sammy and Mark, in many ways are the same,
and they have respect for each other in the game.

OBSERVATIONS AT 4:00 A.M.

Everyone's in bed tucked safely away,
getting ready to start a brand new day.
Everyone is sleeping before a new day will take,
but not me, I'm lying here wide awake.
My cat is sleeping on my bed,
on my leg she rests her gray and white head.
Outside it is still pitch dark,
till the sun comes up and the dogs bark.
Now I'm bored out of my mind,
so I get up and see what I can find.
There's nothing to do, nothing at all,
so I sit here and stare at my wall.
I did not sleep at all through the night,
so I observed everything that was in sight.

I WISH I COULD BE LIKE YOU (DEDICATED TO AMY L.)

You always have a smile even when things go wrong,
I wish I could be like you, positive and strong.
You are one of those people who brightens up others days,
I wish I could be like you, with those uplifting ways.
You do a lot for other people, you give so much,
I wish I could be like you, with a magical touch.
You listen to what others say, and give advice,
I wish I could be like you, it must be nice.
I don't want to be like you in exactly every way,
I am "G" and I never would want to be "A".
Thanks for being such a great role model for me,
if I had to choose someone to copy, you it would be.

GONE, BUT NOT FORGOTTEN (DEDICATED TO AMY L.)

Things just won't be the same without you here,
you always brighten up my night with lots of cheer.
You always listen to me, every time you were there,
what you really did was show me that you do care.
Congratulations on your new job and as you go on your way,
I wish you good luck and I'll think of you every day.
You have taught me a lot that I will never forget,
I am glad you are one of the friends that I have met.
You have taught me about being positive and how to believe,
I will miss you so much when you finally leave.
You are such a great friend, words can't even say,
you will always have a special place in my heart "A".

FRANCIS (DEDICATED TO FRANCIS FIZZAROTTI)

At first when I met you, I loved you so much,
your personality, your smile, your warm touch.
I loved every minute we spent together every day,
but lately, no matter how I try, I don't feel that way.
You didn't do anything, you did nothing wrong,
I know your love for me is still very strong.
For the past two weeks I have been trying like before,
but the worse it is for me, because I can't anymore.
I hate feeling this way, but truthfully I do,
I know you love me, but I can't say I love you.
Everything was fine at the beginning, now it's strange,
I tried to get rid of these bad feelings, nothing would change.
I think we both need space apart from each other for a while,
a separation could be a good idea, like a trial.
But, maybe we should each go our separate ways,
and maybe we will get back together one of these days.

DON'T

Do not speak, don't say a word,
because all I want is to be heard.
Do not try to give me advice,
don't try to make me think twice.
Do not tell me what I should say or do,
because you have no idea what I am going through.
Don't tell me everything will be ok,
because you don't know and so you can't say.
But please don't turn around and hate me,
this is not what I want, can't you see?
All I want you to do is please listen,
think if it were you, what you'd be missin.

THE BEST FRIEND (DEDICATED TO STEPHANIE SMITH)

Our friendship began in fifth grade,
with a promise it would never fade.
As time went on, our friendship had grown strong,
we did a lot of bad stuff that was definitely wrong.
Best friends we soon became,
we had everything in common, everything was the same.
Along came eighth grade,
we were still best friends, it didn't fade.
Then our first year of high school came along,
I had that feeling that something would go wrong.
One day she didn't come to school,
I knew something here just wasn't cool.
She was in the hospital with a brain tumor,
she didn't want this to get around school, like a rumor.
Then a couple of months later, my worst fear,
it got worse, she was in the hospital for half a year.
When she came home she was in a wheelchair, she couldn't walk,
I didn't recognize her, and could hardly see and talk.
When I saw her in that condition, in that chair,
all I could think to myself was why, this isn't fair.
She was like this for another year or so,

I thought the worse was over, but the worse I didn't know.
In the summer I was suppose to go to my aunts, far away,
I didn't want to go, I had a bad feeling when I left that day.
About four days after I was there, it was my birthday,
my dad called, said he had something to say.
The thing I feared most had happened, she died,
she pushed herself to hang on, she really tried.
Now it's over, it's the end,
she will always be my best friend.

A BEST FRIEND NEVER FORGOTTEN (DEDICATED TO STEPHANIE SMITH)

It's been almost two years since you went away,
but I still think of you every single day.
I remember everything about you, the day we met,
you were my best friend, and a person I could never forget.
We did everything together, good and bad,
we stood by each other, whether happy or sad.
I will also not forget the day you died,
all I felt was ripped apart on the inside.
There are plenty of memories we did share,
and as long as I remember them, you will always be there.
Even though it still hurts, and I'm still torn apart,
you are still my best friend, and will always remain in my heart.
I tried to do everything that I could possibly do,
but what could I do to stop this from happening to you?

THE END

When you write for months or even years,
about anything from love to your greatest fears.
The words just seem to naturally come out,
and in your mind, there was never a doubt.
But then something awful happened one day,
you try to write, but there's nothing to say.
Everyone says it's just a writers block,
but it's really an unbreakable lock.
So poetry writing for you is over,
nothing could fix it, not even a four leaf clover.
Writing can become part of you, like a friend,
but it's bad when it comes to a crashing end.

THE END

Sometimes school can be boring, but the years went so fast,
and everyone has special friendships which will forever last.
A good thing to remember is how fun it has actually been,
because you never know if you will see your friends again.
Everyone will be happy to be graduating this year,
especially when they get their diplomas, and their parents cheer.
But in one way or another, everyone is leaving a friend behind,
they will always and forever be in our mind.
Yes as school comes to a close, I can sadly say,
I am leaving a lot of friends behind, and I'll be on my way.
Even though we are all separating, and even though we may part,
all of my friends will always and forever be in my heart.

A NEW FRIEND (DEDICATED TO CHRISTINA)

For the past month, nothing has been going right,
I have been having bad luck every single night.
Until Saturday night, I didn't think anything could help me,
so whatever happened was probably meant to be.
No matter how much I snapped at you, you were still nice,
I wanted you for a friend, I didn't even have to think twice.
I would have been so mad, but there you were with a smile,
gaining your friendship was definitely worthwhile.
Some people think, oh well, friends come and go,
but your friendship is more important to me than you know.
You thanked me for being your friend, but why not?
it made me realize what a great friend I've got.
I'm trying to be a good friend, and I will always be there,
if you're mad or upset, deep inside I do care.
Now I know my days will have a much better start,
a friend as good as you deserves to be in my heart.

A SPECIAL PERSON (DEDICATED TO MRS. CONRAD)

I've watched you teach, coach, and learn,
you help a lot of students and their lives turn.
I wish I would have had you for a teacher last year,
you always have a smile on your face with lots of cheer.
You never seem mad or upsct, even when things go wrong,
I wish I could be like that, I wish I could be that strong.
You are a unique person, there is definitely not another,
and I am sure some day you will make a great mother.
There are many things about you that I admire,
and maybe someday like you, I will make myself higher.
The most important thing which I forgot to say,
you are such a great friend to everyone day by day.

MY WORST FEAR

My mom left my dad over and over again,
she was never home with us where she should have been.
My mom is an alcoholic and would get drunk every night,
I would sit up crying listening to my parents argue and fight.
My mom tried to kill my dad with poison, a gun, and a knife,
I was only seven years old and what a hell of a life.
My mom overdosed on pills and tried to commit suicide,
I guess she felt that no one was on her side.
My parents got divorced and I didn't see her much,
and she promised that she would always stay in touch.
I hated and despised everything she had done, to me she was dirt,
but realizing I still loved her the same is what really made it hurt.
I am twenty now, and she still smokes and drinks every day,
my worst fear is that she is going to die and go away.
My other fear is that some day I will wake up and see,
I have turned into her, the person I really don't want to be.

THE WORST NIGHT

I went into work on a Tuesday night,
me and the manager got into a huge fight.
I tried to clean the bathrooms upstairs,
I tried my best, but no one even cares.
I was told to get plastic bags from the pack,
I got yelled at for taking empty boxes to the back.
I bagged some guys order and left it behind,
by that point I really felt I was losing my mind.
Every time the manager walked by, he gave me a stare,
I got into trouble for something that wasn't fair.
I collected green baskets and put them away,
then they fell over and I didn't know what to say.
So I kicked them hard and hurt my toe,
nothing was going right, I was on a low.
I yelled at the girls in the office, I don't know why,
at that point I just wanted to break down and cry.
I was on my way to freedom, to the door,
I realized I lost my nametag, but nowhere on the floor.
I got home and thought about what happened that night,
what did I do, was it my fault, it just might.
I didn't even know what happened, I wasn't sure,
why did I even act that way for?

ADRIENNE AND RUTHIE

I will never forget anyone as wonderful as you,
I just wish in return, there were something I could do.
I come into work, sometimes not having a very good day,
but you always know exactly the right thing to say.
A lot of times I know you are tired, but still keep a smile,
and that is just one thing that being your friend makes worthwhile.
You make me feel like a very special person inside,
with you, my emotions I do not have to try and hide.
You give me advice, and try to get me to do what is right,
I am grateful and give thanks for you, my friend, every night.
I think you are this great person who had to be,
sent as an angel and a friend to always guide me.

COLLEEN

I thought Redners would be like every other place,
and I knew what I'd be in for and everything to face.
No one would like me because I just didn't fit in,
so many times I was treated like I committed a sin.
They asked you to buddy me, and I thought oh great,
she'll hate me after one or two days, just wait.
But, this was different, I didn't have to dress a certain way,
and I didn't have to worry about how to act or what to say.
It felt great to be accepted just by being me,
you had the qualities of a friend as far as I could see.
Thanks for all your advice, especially on men,
for every problem I've had again and again.
Thanks for giving me a new friend,
such a good friendship you never want to end.
But, of course great things never seem to last,
you are leaving, so everything will be in the past.
Good luck in college and everything you do,
things won't be the same at work without you.

THE HEART

The real and true things come from inside your heart,
but sometimes it is so hard to even know where to start.
A lot of things just naturally come out,
to find other things, you have to search about.
The heart is joyous, knowing you have someone there,
but once in a while it will need a little repair.
Your brain tells you something, your heart not the same,
It's a back and forth battle, like in a tug of war game.
The heart always tells you to do the right things,
and all that matters in the end, is the happiness it brings.
So, when your brain and heart begins to fight,
go for your heart, because it is always right.

HIDDEN LOVE

When I first met you, I had feelings deep inside,
but I can no longer keep them away and let them hide.
The feelings I had, I never had for anyone before,
and each time I saw you they got stronger more and more.
Things happened between us and I don't know why,
and it was the greatest feeling in the world, I can not lie.
I avoided you for a while, because I got afraid,
and I really wish I had just stayed.
I need to know exactly how you feel,
because I know my feelings for you are real.
This next thing might scare you, what I'm about to say,
I've fallen in love with you, and want to be with you every day.

PAIN

He took the scissors and dug all the way down his arm,
the only way to get his feelings out was to do harm.
He ran to the bedroom and pulled the shades all the way down,
and turned all the lights off as he sat there with a frown.
Then the door went shut so no one could get in, so he could be alone,
his friends called but he refused to talk on the phone.
He got into bed and pulled the covers up nice and tight,
things running through his head, like how nothing was going right.
He wanted to stay there forever, didn't want to get out of bed,
and he kept repeating to himself how he wished he were dead.
He thought of overdosing, using a gun or even a knife,
at that point, all he knew is that he really hated his life.
But, here he is still in this world, still breathing in air,
and things still won't go right, nothing will ever be fair.

JACK

At first I thought he was cute, not a big deal,
but as time went on, the stronger I began to feel.
I would have a big smile every time he walked by,
and I would practically melt right after he said hi.
My heart pounds fast whenever he is around,
I see nothing else, and can't even hear a sound.
I decided to get some guts and ask him out,
he said no both times without even a doubt.
Now he knows how I feel, and I feel stupid and dumb,
I act like it doesn't bother me, so in my head I hum.
One night I saw him with someone else in the store,
so I went on 422, blasted radio, and gas pedal to the floor.
I love him so much, and I always will,
I would even shout it to him from the top of a hill.

LOVE

I know what you're thinking, I can read your mind,
you're the best guy in the world that I ever could find.
I know when something is wrong, you don't have to say a word,
you do not have to say anything and you are already heard.
I think of you in the morning and during the day,
your smile, your warmth, your sweet and caring way.
I even think of you as I lye in bed late at night,
counting down the days when you will be holding me tight.
When I am with you, I don't want to let you go,
and it is as hard on you, I truly do know.
I am so much happier now than I was before,
and every day I come to love you so much more.

ALL NIGHT PARTY

I arrived at the house at 10:30 on a Monday night,
the house was easy to miss, but I found it by the light.
We watched Mr. Bean, our favorite comedian on tv,
the room got dark, and we couldn't hardly see.
Then we listened to the radio, N'Sync, and Five,
we got hot, so we were going to take a late night dive.
It was one in the morning and we were still up,
all of a sudden my face was wet from the pup.
Her dad was asleep, so we had to be real quiet,
but we kept laughing, and causing a big riot.
So, here we are the next morning, yawning and tired,
definitely not as hyper as last night, not even wired.

ARE FEELINGS WRONG?

Shutting everyone out is the easiest way to go,
but everyone is asking why, they want to know.
I never have been one to speak up when something is wrong,
I figure I can solve it myself and be very strong.
But, that never happens, and everything is just there,
I start acting different, and think of taking any dare.
Sometimes I drink to make everything go away,
it does, but always winds up coming back to stay.
I want to talk to someone, but I don't know where to begin,
I feel like I've done something wrong, committed some sin.
So, I wait for it to go away, no matter how long,
but, I just don't understand why feeling a way is wrong.

SUMMER

The sun was shining one morning, around seven or eight,
I had gotten a long nights rest, and it really felt great.
The birds were chirping happily away in the trees,
and the flowers were filled with yellow and black bumble bees.
The air was warm with a fresh spring smell,
it was summer time as far as I could tell.
The beach was filled, mostly on the sand,
and you could hear the sound of a band.
All of a sudden, the sky grew dark, and the clouds came,
the coming storm would leave nothing the same.
A tornado ripped through the city and the beach,
everyone was ok, it just went by their reach.
Summer can be very fun when it comes around,
but then there's a storm to always bring it down.

BARNEY

When I first started working, I was on the front end,
and there was this guy bagging, and I knew he'd be my friend.
He helped me to fit in, I felt so relaxed, it was great,
he was always on time for work, he was never once late.
His sense of humor was the best of anyone else around,
I was so happy and lucky for the new friend I had found.
His wit was also great, and you could surely bet,
there was more to him, I hadn't seen the best part yet.
He knew when to get serious, and he knows when to have fun,
he always had a smile on his face and said bye when his day was done.
He always told me jokes, while at the register I stood,
if I could show him how much he meant, I really would.
Now I find out that he is sick and I feel bad,
bad things happening to good people just makes me mad.
I will now try to help him, just as he has helped me,
because Barney is the greatest guy there could ever be.
My thoughts are with him, and his special magical touch,
and he is missed here dearly, very very much.

THE BEST PRESENT (DEDICATED TO DENISE ROSSI)

On your first day of work, you wanted everything to go right,
and I knew you would be one of my friends by the end of the night.
I said hi to you, and I really didn't know you that well,
but you were a nice person, as far as I could tell.
I hoped you would like me, I didn't see why not,
and I knew I was lucky for the new friend I had got.
I always give my new friends something they won't forget,
so I gave you a hug, the best present I have ever given yet.
You liked your present, and that's when I knew,
the best present I could get was a friend like you.
Your friendship means more to me than I can say,
and as long as you are my friend, I know I will be ok.

I REMEMBER YOU ALWAYS
(DEDICATED TO MISS LOOSE)

I had you for History class my freshman year,
failing that class was my biggest fear.
You helped me out, you got me through,
and I got an A because of you.
You always made things seem ok,
and I loved to pass you in the hall every day.
You just weren't a teacher, you were a friend,
and I was thankful for you, when all my days would end.
There are just some people who touch my life a lot,
you are one of them, and in my heart will have a special spot.
When I come to visit the school, and you're not there,
I will think of you always, I will always care.

SUE
(DEDICATED TO
SUE SABOLICK)

As soon as I met you, right away I just knew,
a great friend you would become, one of my very few.
I guess it was your friendly voice, your friendly ways,
a person who would brighten up all of my worst days.
You were someone I could talk to, someone who was there,
most importantly, you showed me that you did care.
I adopted you as my mom, that is how much you mean to me,
you were the greatest friend you could ever possibly be.
I was hoping that you would never have to leave,
and now you are, and it is just so hard to believe.
So, you told me your last day is Saturday,
and I promise it will be special in every possible way.
Just remember that you are always in my heart,
and I will love you always, even though we may part.

TRUE OR NOT?

Someone told me you're as beautiful as you feel,
and the beauty inside is what's true and real.
But, I feel no beauty inside or even out,
my mind is so full of every possible doubt.
My boyfriend got made fun of because of me,
I never realized I caused him that much misery.
Why he is even still with me, I really don't know,
I think sometimes he really wants to let me go.
He says he loves me for who I am inside,
but there are just a lot of things from him I hide.
He refuses to let me go, he still holds on and tries,
but I don't know if he means it, or if it's a pack of lies.

A NEW BEGINNING

My boyfriend and I broke up one day,
I started drinking to make the pain go away.
I lost my best friend when she died,
after all this, I just wanted to disappear and hide.
I got fired from my job on a Monday night,
I dropped out of college, nothing was going right.
I thought I had lost all my friends from three years,
and that was the biggest of all my fears.
My boyfriend and I got back together, it was great,
it just proves that love is never too late.
I got a new job and was making money, much more,
I wanted to work there every day, in this big store.
I stopped drinking and got back into school,
part time was not good enough, so I went full.
The best part is that I still have my friends, everyone,
just because I don't work with him, our friendship doesn't
have to be done.

FAR APART, BUT CLOSER THAN EVER (DEDICATED TO STEPHANIE SMITH)

I yell at my boyfriend for saying your name,
without you around, things will never be the same.
I can't even look at your picture and I start to cry,
I have a lot of unanswered questions, but the biggest is why.
When you died three years ago, to me it was the end,
but I will never replace you as my best friend.
I missed your funeral, because I was hours away,
but I still feel I should have been there on that one day.
I will never say good-bye to you, I don't think I can,
all I have now is memories of how our friendship began.
Every day I think about you, and the way things should be,
things will never be the same for you or me.

REDNERS

Richard is the funny guy out of everyone,
he does his job well and still has lots of fun.
Carolyn was my trainer, and she is very polite,
she knows how to take the wrong things and make them right.
I come into work and there is Cathy, always with a smile,
and that puts me into a better mood, even for a little while.
Kathy can brighten up a darkest day,
with her energetic and spontaneous way.
Jackie is a person that anyone would admire,
lots of friends, being herself, and her way to inspire.
Jack is the cute one, I have to look when he walks by,
but if he would ever find out, I think I would die.

PRESSURE

I wake up in the morning and I am tired,
very unlike me, I am usually energetic and wired.
I run around the house and try to get everything clean,
but I try to do too much for only being a teen.
I work forty hours a week, and sometimes more,
sometimes I don't know why I do these things for.
I have to fit my poetry writing in, so my book will be done,
some days I don't even have time to fit any fun.
In the fall I start college, more stress,
sometimes I like this, I just have to confess.
Taking deep breaths is a way to try and calm down,
but sometimes it doesn't work and the pressure stays around.

THE OCEAN

The air was calm, not a cloud up in the sky,
and the sun shined so brightly from way up high.
The sand was as hot as a red burning fire,
but the beach seemed to be everyone's greatest desire.
There were people lying on the sand, walking on the board walk,
some just preferred to listen to their music, or even talk.
The water was at a warm temperature, it was just right,
but it would get much cooler as darkness leads into night.
The shallow end was filled with children, ages three to five,
they had not learned how to swim yet and definitely not dive.
The waves were mainly out in the deep end of the ocean,
and they will come in and out in a relaxing swaying motion.

THINGS HAPPEN FOR A REASON

I watched him as he talked to his friends, as he stood there,
I realized that there was a part of me for him that still did care.
He was my ex-boyfriend, we had been apart for about a year,
and my heart started pounding as towards me he started to get near.
I snapped out of that fantasy, as my boyfriend called my name,
but for this guy my feelings just weren't the same.
He pulled me towards him, so with my ex I lost eye contact,
I still loved Shawn, and that was nothing but a true fact.
As Shawn was getting ready to leave, he came over to me and we hugged,
and I could tell that this really had Francis bugged.
Four months later Shawn and I were back together again,
this is just the way it should have always been.
Every time we broke up, we always got back some other day,
it's all because we were meant to always be this way.

POPEYE

He sat at baseball games and cheered loud,
whenever he was around, there was never a cloud.
He sat at basketball games, and gave each girl a high five,
even with his sickness, he couldn't be anymore alive.
He sat at Wrestling matches, and was the biggest fan,
all I can say is I will miss this man.
He use to come into Genuardi's and give me a hug every night,
he knew how to make one of my bad days right.
When Popeye died, it was a very sad day
everyone will remember him, each in their own way.
Popeye is gone, but his memory will always live,
and how much he went through and still had to give.

THERE ARE SOME THINGS

There are some things a guy should never say,
like why do you wear your hair that way?
There are some things a guy should never do,
like stealing his parents car just to impress you.
There are some names a guy should never use,
it would be considered verbal and emotional abuse.
There are some things a guy should definitely say,
like, my aren't you looking pretty today.
There are some things a guy should definitely do,
like bring flowers and just to say I love you.
There are some names a guy should definitely use,
pet names, or little lovable names they choose.

ALWAYS IN MY HEART (DEDICATED TO SUE MCCANDLESS)

I will never forget the first day we met,
you were nice, but I hadn't seen the best yet.
Our friendship took off faster than I could believe,
you are one friend I definitely didn't want to leave.
I could tell you anything, good or bad,
and you could always tell if I was happy or sad.
One day I found out you were leaving the store,
nothing would ever be as it was before.
It turned out that I would see you every day,
we were in the same school, and I walked your way.
Then I graduated and we were separated once again,
nothing was going as it should have been.
I came to visit, but that wasn't very much,
the last thing I wanted was for us to lose touch.
I will always consider you as my greatest friend,
and for our friendship, there will be no end.
I think of you often, whether if we are close or apart,
you are always and forever in my heart.

EXPRESS SHOP ADVENTURES

I was sitting in the express shop on a Monday night,
it was slow and there wasn't a customer in sight.
The cigarettes were filled, that didn't have to be done,
I had to find something to do to have at least a little fun.
So, I collected the red baskets and put them all away,
right by the door in the metal basket tray.
Then I cleaned my counter top down so it would look nice,
I was desperate for something to do, so I went over it twice.
Then a customer came to my line, and so did a lot more,
next thing I knew, they were backed up all the way to the door.
All at once they disappeared once again,
and there was an empty space where they had once been.
I was counting down the time till I could go home, about an hour,
I might as well relax, because I didn't have much strength or power.
So, my adventures at the Express Shop were coming to an end,
but I would definitely be back there soon again.

THE REAL WORLD

Things are a lot different since school is done,
many cannot wait, but it's not really fun.
Everything changes so fast once you graduate,
for some it means relaxing, partying, and sleeping late.
I have to study at least eight hours a night,
I hardly have time to do my favorite thing, write.
I work at least forty hours a week, sometimes more,
by Sunday night I am run down and wore.
I don't have any contact with my friends ever,
but I will not forget them, they will be with me forever.
This is definitely a very big change for me,
but in the end, a successful person I will be.

THE MILLENIUM

As we come to the end of the year, we look back on many things,
but we re also looking at the future and what it brings.
As the ball drops on New Years Eve, some will be hiding under the chair,
they fear the world will end, so they have to beware.
There were great people like J.F.K. jr. who unfortunately died,
but we would still be remembered the same even if he had survived.
Hitler is someone no one will want to remember in the New Year,
he brought violence and hatred into people, even fear.
Many people will try to make a name for themselves, good or bad,
and it might bring happiness to people, or make them sad.
The Millenium is the biggest event that will happen for everyone,
and some don't care, but others will have extreme fun.

I WISH (DEDICATED TO LISA CAPPERELLA)

I wish there were something I could say,
but it is impossible for me to make things ok.
I wish I could make your pain disappear,
I can't, but I will always be here.
I wish there were something I could do,
I can't, but I will always be here for you.
I lye awake late at night,
wishing things for you could be alright.
I can only imagine the pain you feel,
and the worst part is, this is real.
I guess I should bring this poem to an end,
remember, you will always have me as a friend.

ENOUGH OR NOT? (DEDICATED TO LISA CAPPERELLA)

I am trying to make things a little bit alright,
so I buy you everything you might like in sight.
I bought you flowers, but they will just die,
so I thought of other things I could buy.
I bought you a few cards, still not enough,
so I went out to look for some more stuff.
I found a stuffed animal, a cute bear,
but the dogs might chew it, and it would tear.
I wrote you a poem, at least I tried my best,
I still needed to give more, so where would I get the rest?
Then I realized what you needed wasn't in a store,
it was a friend, a hug, and not much more.
I hope my conclusions are at least a little right,
but, if they are stupid, then I'm sorry for my bad insight.

A BIRTHDAY WISH (DEDICATED TO LISA CAPPERELLA)

I don't want a party or even a car,
I don't want a vacation and to travel far.
I don't want clothes, and I don't want money,
and no this isn't a joke, it's not supposed to be funny.
I don't want a stereo or even a phone,
I don't care if I spend my birthday all alone.
I don't want jewelry or anything like that,
I don't want a dog, rabbit, hamster, or cat.
There is one thing that I want for this special day,
I really want my friend Lisa's pain to go away.
Taking away her hurt is a good enough present for me,
and it is a wish that may or may not come to be.

GOODBYE, AGAIN (DEDICATED TO COLLEEN CURTIN)

You never appreciate a good friend until they go away,
saying good-bye is a word you just don't want to say.
You left for college about two weeks ago,
how much I would miss you, I just didn't know.
The final good-bye as I headed for the door,
the final moment right there in front of the store.
I didn't cry in front of you, I had to be strong,
because if I had made you cry, that would have been wrong.
A week went by and I missed you so much,
but we e-mailed each other and stayed in touch.
It just wasn't the same, we were so far apart,
but one thing was for sure, you were still close to my heart.
Every day I wished you would come back,
I would even give up my crush on Jack.
You came back for vacation, just for Labor Day,
and I wished that you could just stay.
But you are going back soon, and again I'll cry,
and the worst part in the whole thing is saying good-bye.

THE BRIGHTER SIDE OF A BAD NIGHT (DEDICATED TO CHRISTINA)

On Sunday you had a very bad night,
not much seemed to be going right.
Maybe someone said something they just shouldn't say,
but I will be behind you all the way.
Maybe someone did something they just shouldn't do,
but don't let it get you down, I still believe in you.
Maybe someone was just treating you bad,
and they pushed you too far and you got mad.
Perhaps it was none of these and you were just tired,
nothing could revive you, no chance of getting wired.
Whenever you are having a bad day, remember one thing,
think of the happiness to others that you bring.

A SPECIAL PERSON (DEDICATED TO MANIAC)

I was sitting in History class, my mind wandering away,
thinking about meeting you someday.
I met you on the computer and I got to know you,
you were going to be a special person, somehow I just knew.
We sent each other stuff as much as we could,
and we wanted to meet each other, and we knew we would.
I hated to get off the computer, I didn't want to say goodbye,
I couldn't wait until I was back on again just to say hi.
I missed you so much, a feeling I have had never,
I feel like I have known you for a while, actually forever.
Unfortunately our distance was keeping us apart,
but you are still close to me, right in my heart.

I'M SORRY
(DEDICATED TO CHRISTINA)

I'm sorry if I'm in a bad mood every night,
I'm sorry if I argue and put up a fight.
I'm sorry if I yell at you or get real loud,
I'm sorry if I seem like I'm floating on a cloud.
I'm sorry for acting weird and zoning out,
I'm sorry for getting a look on my face that you wonder about.
I'm sorry for the things I may do day by day,
I'm sorry for ignoring you and not knowing what to say.
I'm sorry for crying in front of you,
I don't want to lose my great friend, one of my very few.

SUE
(DEDICATED TO
SUE FROM REDNERS)

When I first saw you, I thought uh-oh not again,
things will always be as they have always been.
You would dislike me, without even knowing me,
but that wasn't the case, and soon I came to see.
You gave me a smile and a friendly hi,
but it would probably last one day and then good-bye.
I was wrong, you hung around and helped me out,
I wasn't sure what caused this good thing to come about.
So I didn't question things, and left everything the way it was,
it is such a great feeling in what making a new friend does.
I didn't talk much because I was afraid of saying something wrong,
but it was just me being paranoid all along.
It didn't really matter, because deep inside I knew,
another friend was added to my heart, and it was you.
Now you are going to college somewhere far away,
and I'll never forget when you gave me a new friend on that one day.
To some a friend is not a big deal, easy to get,
but not for me, and so you are a friend I'll never forget.

BAD LUCK
(DEDICATED TO CHRISTINA)

You did not have very good luck on Thursday night,
everything went wrong, nothing went right.
Most of it was because of me, that I know,
if only I didn't have my screen so low.
You went to adjust it and hit the wrong key,
and got yelled at by a customer because of me.
Your finger is still bruised from when I slammed it in the drawer,
and I know it still hurts, it's probably still sore.
You had to do a refund but couldn't get it straight,
what other bad luck would I bring you, what fate?
A soda can sprung a leak all over the place,
and then I saw the look on your face.
I felt so bad about everything I did to you,
I am very sorry, and don't know what else to do.
All I wanted was a new friend,
but my bad luck has probably brought it to an end.

I WISH YOU WERE HERE (DEDICATED TO STEPHANIE SMITH)

I sit in class and think, you should be there,
you should be in that empty spot of that chair.
I go to work, and you should be standing next to me,
all there is, is an empty spot where you would be.
I go out driving, and I think you should be too,
still that empty space and nothing I can do.
I go to the mall and see other friends all over the place,
but there I am again, and next to me, an empty space.
Sometimes I feel bad doing this stuff, because you're not here,
you are still my best friend no matter how far, or how near.
So whenever I get sad because you're not there,
it's mainly because life just isn't fair.

SOMETIMES

Sometimes I feel like the world is against me,
even though that's not the way it should be.
Sometimes I get this feeling deep inside,
and I just want to disappear and hide.
Sometimes things build up more and more,
and I don't know why I let them get that way for.
Sometimes I let people get me upset over stupid things,
if only they knew how much pain it actually brings.
Sometimes I am filled with guilt, because of things I do,
if only some people would understand, if only they knew.
Sometimes everything is too much and I break down and cry,
everything gets messed up, not matter how hard I try.

ANDY KAUFFMAN

As a child he pretended to have his own sport's show,
but no one knew what he would be when he would grow.
When he did, he played small night clubs around the town,
he wasn't very popular and a lot of people put him down.
His most popular show was doing the Elvis Presley impression,
George Shapiro set up a meeting with him, a 10 minute session.
Andy was very popular now, especially for his "tank you vedy much",
he was always washing his hands after anything he would touch.
Andy's next big show was singing along to Mighty Mouse,
a little while after, he had a wife, and his own house.
Andy had another side to him that no one knew about,
he was also a guy named Tony Clifton, which eventually got out.
Transforming back and forth, the people loved these two,
not many people hated them, there was very few.
Andy was always doing jokes, no one knew when he was telling the truth,
he was just getting started, he was still in his time of youth.
One night Andy said he had an announcement that would shock everyone,
he had cancer and his career would soon be over with, it would be done.
His last show was the biggest one, at Carnigee Hall,
right after that is when he hit the biggest down fall.

The Chemo therapy wasn't working, and he lost all of his hair,
everyone was upset, they just didn't think it was fair.
Andy died days after his last performance, but left a big trace,
and a song was played, "The World is Such a Wonderful Place".

Printed in the United States
779000003B